I0223587

THE WORLD SINCE YESTERDAY

Poems by
Will Walker

BLUE LIGHT PRESS ◆ 1ST WORLD PUBLISHING

1ˢᵗ WORLD
PUBLISHING

SAN FRANCISCO ◆ FAIRFIELD ◆ DELHI

The World since Yesterday
Copyright ©2025 by Will Walker

All rights reserved. Printed in the United States of America. No part of this book may be used or reproduced in any manner whatsoever without written permission except in the case of brief quotations embodied in critical articles and reviews. For information contact:

1st World Library
PO Box 2211
Fairfield, IA 52556
www.1stworldpublishing.com

Blue Light Press
www.bluelightpress.com
bluelightpress@aol.com

Book & Cover Design
Melanie Gendron
melaniegendron999@gmail.com

Author Photo
Valerie Walker

First Edition

Library of Congress Cataloging-in-Publication Data

ISBN: 978-1-4218-3570-9

Acknowledgements

Some of these poems have previously been published in these versions or slightly different versions in *Common Ground Review, Euphony, Jet Fuel Review, Map Literary, Mudlark, Nimrod International Journal, Parcel, Salamander, Soundings East,* and *Southern Poetry Review.*

For Valerie, always

Oh, when I get it right, will you tell me please?
Joan Armatrading

Table of Contents

I.

II.

III.

IV.

I.

What Remains

The desert silence
is punctuated by the scratchings
of a few dusty lizards,
croak of a passing raven,
and surprising lines of rocks
arranged by the locals
just off the highway
to send a simple message:
proof of life, and its fondness
for alcohol after midnight.

That same arid absence
is an empty opening
to endless surprise,
an invitation
to levitate, to float gently
upward toward the stratosphere
and view this jeweled planet
from the undisturbed
stillness of the pockmarked moon.

Filled with constant regard
it faces earth unceasingly,
a worshipful satellite
never tiring of the little swirls
of tornadoes and hurricanes,
the sudden silent eruptions
of the largest volcanoes,
the delicate plumes of ash
extending featherlike
over the azure oceans,
shadowing the edges of continents
littered with fossils
of the dinosaurs.

Benediction

Just keeping watch has gotten me this far,
and I hope farther, to this day and its prospect
of ordered anonymity, the delicious place
of a citizen drinking too much coffee,

strolling through the Panhandle
goosing his dormant metabolism
as he passes a passel of bums convened
on their favorite sunstruck bench, where they sit
twisted on that nameless brand of malt liquor

that makes them feel like matinee idols riding high
in the old West. No booze before breakfast,
that's my creed, stay friendly with the voices
in my head, the ones that claim to be Buddha
or Jesus or their neatly dressed emissaries—

and the ones that urge violence on my relatives,
incarceration of the loud and bug-ridden: Listen
with respect to their anger, and honor their outrage.
They've earned their place, though theirs are solutions
only embraced by wing nuts and the sad, addled souls
who never learned to count to ten, who couldn't sit still
till recess—wild and dangerous and unbroken.

Insomnia

Each thought a dragon that grows
by the minute, while the St. George
of your resolve champs at the bit
to engage with lance, broadsword, and shield.

Counting sheep is never a strategy,
except for the shepherd who can name them
and imagine steering their vacancies
away from the edges of steep ravines.

Organize alphabetically the many pleasures
of life—art, bread, and cheese—
or search for nouns that also serve as verbs—
air, beat, cheat—and let your body sing

the cellular song of reconstruction,
repair your decrepit metropolis
with the miracle of sleep, the balm that waits
behind your darting, unseeing eyes.

Scapegoat

The annoying fake clock on the rustic armoire
to my right: I blame it for its fake ticking
and faux brass finish. It's a piece of plastic
whose little chandelier of balls twists
with a battery assist and tick-tocks as if it had works,
a delicate clockmaker's soul keeping time
for the aimless folk nearby. It's a phony,

a cheap wedding gift from the chain-smoking mother
of a former friend whose voice hasn't soiled
our old-fashioned answering device
on our old-fashioned landline for decades.

I should hurl it at the wall and curse the whole family
for their fondness for plaster of Paris cupids
and Amaretto. To say nothing of their fiscal improprieties.

But there would be consequences.
I'd have to pick up the pieces
and explain my rage, a tiny whirlwind
keening for justice and retribution,
pure abstracts in a world of fake clocks
and false promises, grifters and crooks.

In the Shower

Soaping my left bicep with my right hand
and a small bar of sandalwood soap
the color of cinnamon,
for a minute I am David—not so much
the cut physique, eternal
sharp-eyed youth taking a bead
on destiny, God's righteous instrument—

but the naked part, and the chosen one,
though only marked to startle for a moment
with the bright thought of the body's
miraculous being, each movement
a ballet of synapses activating muscles
and bones, supported by a river of blood
bathed in oxygen from lungs
driven by nerves that never sleep
or take the afternoon off,

but flex the diaphragm with a directive
that says Live long and prosper,
oh common triumph of biology
and evolution, the so-called paragon
of animals, nearly hairless biped
with the strange dangling appendage
and unfortunate bald spot,
you are this morning's nominee
for the electric Crown of Creation.

And then it's just my astonished

thoughtful hand soaping my untoned
but still meaty upper arm, muscles
that, though nameless, rise
to every simple task, and skin
that glories in its surprising smoothness,
its permeable wetness, and the scent
of an exotic but not uncommon spice.

A Short History of Flowers

Hammurabi loved flowers
and strewed his bridal bed
with rose petals, blood red.

Nero loved the fuchsia
for attracting hummingbirds
and their delectable tongues.

Louis XIV sent Madame de Maintenon
lilies, though he smelled
like a bedraggled billy goat.

All the wrong people love flowers,
which have no politics,
speak of nothing inconvenient,

and seduce with the most
complicated palette.
That they are defenseless

makes them so alluring.
That they surprise
with the mystery of scent,

spicy to sweet. That they die
petal by petal,
surrendering to gravity,

and rot like lovers

peeling off a glove
or yielding to the spell of time.

Hitler himself was fond
of purple tulips and offered them
to Eva Braun before their first kiss.

Tools of the wicked
we might call them,
though doesn't the hydrangea

speak up to defend
its multifaceted blossom,
wouldn't lilac wrap its perfume

around a manifesto
and implore us
to extend asylum?

Sight-Reading

Now and then I lose my place.
The group plays on
while I sit, bow in hand,
cello at the ready,
and stare at the staves
of notes that no longer
fit. I have a script,
but no cue.

Like those conversations that drift
into politics while you sit
and listen to the angry solo
about something so remote
your dinner partner might as well
be playing a bassoon,
or jamming with his one note
in somebody's unheard,
scratchy blues chorus
in the middle of an evening
of Mozart.

And then the talk turns
to movies or the excellence
of strawberry shortcake
and you nod again in time
with the others, as though
you haven't just returned
from a brief sojourn
in a gulag so remote

you don't even know
the names of the strange seabirds
circling overhead, or the creatures
something like badgers
stripping bark off the rotten log
just ahead on the straggling
path that led you here,
an endless tundra
so far from home.

II.

Many Years Ago

The young man is burning his papers.
He does not think they are poems.
He does not think he is a poet.
He thinks they are records of his many failures.
He has lost faith in so many things.
Maybe even fire.

Still, he burns the pile slowly,
so many sheets, so many words,
so many pieces.
He has no hope for the paper
or the words.

He listens to the crackling
and watches the gray smoke.
He smells the match and sees the little glow.
He feels his failure rise up the chimney
that is such a solid, workmanlike construction,
and so indifferent.

The words rise into the overcast skies.
It is winter. At the piles of birdseed
out of sight on the terrace,
the chickadees flock
to feed. Though it is winter,
they do not wait for spring.

Another Tired Ode to Spring

Honey, she says—

                (I hate it when she calls me honey,
like she's some honky-tonk crooner in a gin mill
in St. Louis just through singing "I Want a Hotdog
for My Roll" the way it's meant to be sung, low-down
and dirty)—

                Honey, she says—

                      (not like a decent muse,
trained in the classical arts, experienced in prophesy,
talking in tongues, a goddamn inspiration
on any continent, in any age, even the present
corrupted digital troglodyte era of the serious
jabbering into the thin air about their alleged
stock options)—

                    Give. It. A. Rest.

And she's right. Yes, the world
may be ending. It's earthquake weather.
Fanatics want to incinerate you for the crime
of drawing breath, and the globe is twitching
with changes that will knock you on your ass.

But put off the bellyache a day and enjoy the joggers
in their spandex underwear and bouncing ponytails,
striding toward the future like it might be cataclysm
free and filled with that most nebulous
of ethers, promise, lurking in the scrawny lilacs
even here, a city where they barely bloom.

Unannounced

Last night a man flew
into my own flying dream and touched
my hand, confirming our flight

as real and slowed my trajectory
into the ionosphere.
We almost talked, the wordless way

that dreams supply some truth
without a lexicon, uncertain clarity,
the telling mist of morning light.

And (back on earth) I toured his house,
from which he was missing, and his yacht—
so clean, so white.

And his message—inscrutable and vivid,
a flying being with a very physical hand,
lighter than thought, yet anchoring me again

to someplace mundane
and earthbound, South Florida perhaps,
a seaside town, and a particular life

of dazzling precision, from which
he has disappeared
without a trace.

Morning Brew

It's the coffee, helping you imagine
the morning is bright and full of promise.

That towering delightful cumulus of projects
may burn off by noon, forcing you

to seek the shade of some untroubled tree—
eucalyptus, cedar, bottlebrush, monkey puzzle,

anything tall and green will do—
and pull out a sandwich to console yourself.

But the bustle of useless mental hijinks
is going well, so well you know things will develop

in some startling revelation: Jesus, perhaps,
will smile at you from a passing bus, or Buddha

in his corpulent enlightened fat man incarnation
will waddle by and offer you part of his chocolate donut,

and you will smile and say, *No thanks, I'm sticking
with my raisin bagel*, and he will nod,

bright-eyed, while you flourish your half-
eaten bagel and kvell with pride to be loitering

on that street corner as if you're a full-time flâneur
in Paris—*très chic!* Or you're about to lecture

at a nearby lycée on the troubadours
and their code of courtly love and purified passion,

spawning insanely high-strung rhyming ballads
plucked on lutes and other odd gourd-shaped instruments.

The blood! The drama! The roses!

On the Cutting Edge

Every man is wanted, and no man
is wanted much.
                    —Ralph Waldo Emerson

Today my task is simple: Walk
two miles; raise my metabolism
in the name of any favorite saint or my health plan;
contemplate my place in the universe
and pick up a drifting sheet of sky-blue tissue
to recycle. Notice the crossing guard,

decked out in his striking orange vest,
stepping into the road to tell the silence
STOP for longer than needed, enjoying
his moment in the street for something more
than only what it is, then back to the curb
while he listens to the rush of stillness
on the empty boulevard.

The Lessons of History

You open the front door and call out
I'm home! to the impassive silence,
surprising and uninterrupted.
Your wife and two dogs have adjourned,
you note, leaving you alone with yourself
and the house, bereft of status.

Once a husband and steward, now a man
in a house that is daydreaming
of its own indifferent past—the fireman
who built it over a century ago,
the quiet neighborhood in which it settled,
its undistinguished history, and the strange interlude

when the young tarted the place up,
painted it in Day-Glo, smoked too much pot
and, if they were worth their salt,
fucked their brains out, leaving behind
the fading odor of sage, a disheveled aura
of visionary aftermath, and wiring

compromised enough to rain a startling
shower of sparks on your terrified wife.
That was before the men with hammers
upgraded every system in the house.

Since then, just you and your wife
and a cavalcade of pets,
going on now thirty years. No amount
of attention to the roof or yard has kept
the years from passing.

And Yet Good News

Nothing lasts. Cities crumble. Whole civilizations
close up shop. The rosebuds so favored
in verse: Woe is us. And yet good news:

Your grief will end. The universe and its short
attention span will release some little ecstasy.
If not the rosebuds, then some old, tired joke.

Sunset may light the sky. You may hit a high C
while wailing with your dogs. Or stumble
into the storied, expansive present, where breath

is hallowed and dirt is fertile, and rocks are so stolid
they seem genial—dependable, persuasive, anonymous—
and green is the color of all thought

leafing before your eyes, and the fountain of your heart
is in love with its own smooth muscle
and that science project that pushes oxygen

into your tiny capillaries. Your breath: the sacred wind
that animates a forum filled with baseball scores
and snippets of immortal verse, recollections of passion

so intense the lights went out, all circuits blown. You will rise,
light as air, and bathe in the spark of galaxies millions of years
gone. You will cross the road. Because you want to.

III.

Why Am I Here?

You know it's the wrong question to ask
on a rainy morning in February, because the only answer
the state will readily suggest till spring is this:
to pay taxes, my son. You have to pony up,

to fill the coffers we empty on explosions
halfway around the world.
But take satisfaction in your role as tiny technocrat,
boil water for simple beverages, crumple the news

of the day into a useless wad to give the recyclers work,
adjust the thermostat to run up today's gas bill,
flick on a light in service of the power company.
Not everyone can be a plutocrat, shaking fortunes

from the pockets of millions. We don't all get
that well-lit close-up in a coherent plot of espionage
and derring-do. Sometimes the short days
just end in darkness.

The Land of the Free

Are you a good American?
asks the shopping cart jockey in the park,
accosting a chestnut-haired six-year-old
on a pink bicycle, Peter Max flowers stuck
on the fenders, and pink streamers
dangling from the handlebars.

Then he moves on, and the girl waits
for her mother, her tidy white
safety helmet fastened
on her shampooed head.
Someday we'll have an answer
from this tiny bicyclist,

but today her community covers
ten blocks, and her only thought
is to ride home in time for cookies and milk.
For a few more years, this lucky girl
won't even understand the question.

Sunday

Sometimes there's guidance in the horoscope.
Or an obituary provides a tiny spark:
a life well-lived, filled with adventure, love,
or a deep devotion to tropical fish.

The Style page offers no help beyond new variations
on the old theme: Change your outfit,
change your life! Buy a new lamp
as a conversation piece! As for an actual Sabbath,
a deep draught from some crystal fountain:

That's not news. The shade tree outside
my front door could preach a better sermon
about roots and the grace of God
replenishing the ground water, fouled as it may be.

And I, perhaps, could preach more persuasively
about stewardship, caring for what is given,
learning what elements support growth,
what the seasons promise us all.

A little bit of water, a dash of sun, doses
of cleansing rain. And perhaps a pagan sense
of wonder, watching the way we hurry
this way and that while the tree tells time
by seasons and stands pat, as if satisfied.

Life and Other Mysteries

Life is reduced to inconvenient logistics:
Put on your pants one leg at a time,
giving extra attention to that interlude
when you stand on your bum right leg and pray.

What's the use? Today is the sandwich wrapper
once you've eaten your turkey on whole wheat.
Beauty is overpriced. Except, the poet thinks, for poetry,
which no one buys. Perhaps, he thinks, it's time

to veer toward variety—an interlude of juggling,
a strange costume, declamation and oratory;
a little couldn't hurt. Some new
material: an ode to salami, or toothpicks,

or the timeless appeal of almonds. The genealogy
of fleas. Volcanoes I have known. The humor of tomatoes.
The long migration of the monarchs. Perfumes
of the Middle Ages. The body language of hummingbirds.

Ode to a Meteorologist

For Roberta Gonzalez

Every weekday evening
you step on screen
and deliver. Not quite
goddess of weather,
more a stage mother
of isobars, a cheerleader
of highs and lows,
a forecaster of the future
we all pretend
to manage.

In this version of tomorrow
and the week ahead, the fronts
sweep through with unrestrained
abandon and a passel
of gab about the radar
and the temps,
precipitation and ski conditions,
sun and clouds,
the occasional miraculous
thunderstorm, all
ushered into our living room
with good cheer by a gal
dressed, one might suppose,
for a night on the town.

Our days: not quite soap opera—
no bastard sons of weather fronts,
no bands of tropical depressions

defrauding the coast
or ripping off that naive
forest of firs—
but not quite myth,
no prophecy told in gnomic couplets,
no empires hanging on the giddy utterances
of the keepers of the mystery.

Roberta cheers us, gives science
a good name, chortles about
her satellites and the high cumulus,
gives prophecy a new,
saleable niche: Tomorrow, she coos,
and tomorrow, and tomorrow:
wind! rain! sun! cloudy
on the coast! morning mist!

Not What I Want to Hear

Keep your needs simple (I tell myself)
and you'll be disappointed less.
No elevator to the stars, no penthouse
on the moon, no ski chalet in the high
purple mountains nor a cabana by a tropic shore.

Even those who love you will disappoint
when you ask for fabulous. Some, though,
may offer sympathy for your many losses, or step
to hold the door at the scene of your most recent
disappointment. Waiters may smile when delivering
soup, and even the most vigilant of cops may let you
slip through a yellow in the rain. Love is often

too much to ask. You may as well tell your little niece
to be Rembrandt. Courtesy, on the other hand,
is a small bouquet of daisies, often in reach.
Sunshine in the afternoon is less than your name
in lights, and yet sufficient till dusk.

3:00 a.m.

To my left, the Big Dipper, upside down,
        points to the North Star somewhere
                in our neighbor's Victorian living room.

The houses of this enclosed block
        are all the color of night.
                Is this the afterlife of the Greeks,

that shadowland from which all shades
        yearn to escape for even a second
                of sun, the smell of cocoa

in a favorite cup, the slightest touch
        of a loved one's fingertip?
                My dog is sure this yard is still

the plot of scents, the place
        to void when sleep breaks,
                her turf at all hours.

I'm exiled in my own home.
        Even the House of Fun
                has a basement filled with the smell

of stale beer and crushed cigarettes
        and cold sweat. The Dipper
                lets me know where to look

for Sirius. That much I know.

Where to look for redemption
for the dead or love

from the living—well, not the Lode Star,
not the silence of 3:00 a.m.
Not my dog's hobbled steps

hauling her tired carcass
back inside. The redwood
next door, all feathered darkness,

has grown fifty years alone
without a hoedown and seems
willing to go a couple hundred more.

IV.

Out with the Old

Imagine Zeus after plastic surgery,
flexing his enhanced pecs, gaze no longer stern
and forbidding, but frozen in taut-skinned
bewilderment, half god, half mannequin,
trying to hurl a thunderbolt at some offending mortal.
Or Athena, decked out with the pert breasts
available for the cost of a Caribbean vacation,
trying to embody wisdom.

Perhaps our gods are meant to fade.

Nobody views the Sphinx and turns to his wife,
concerned, to say *She needs work*. If time wastes
all things, why not the gods, consigned
to their special rest homes in history books,
when randy pagan titans hid behind every bush,
in rut, and the world was filled with their mutant offspring.

Hangover

All plans scuttled.
A whole fleet of activities foundered.

Sunlight an insult. The joyful cries
of children: anathema. Even the dogs

seem to slink by, aware I'd rather
kick than pat their scrawny pelts.

On my daily walk, I count
the steps till I can stop.

The body labors, an overworked
blood factory straining

out the toxins the only way
it knows how, molecule by molecule.

And the mind gets busy with recrimination,
saying what minds say to keep busy:

If only you'd thought of this last night,
if only you'd reminded yourself

that tomorrow would come and you
would still be here, squinting, cursing,

and reciting that foolish litany of promises
to your burdened liver, toiling kidneys,

churning stomach, your knotted brain,
while day, unfazed, carries on and on.

Many Are Called

That car alarm blaring but faint—
somewhere down the block, around the corner—
could almost be a church bell (it's a Sunday,

about the time they summon us to worship,
though few now heed the call). But mindless,
insistent, seeming to want to sound all morning,

an appliance blowing its own horn to no end,
a one-note no-talent solo. The noise
makes you want to grab a crowbar

and smash a windshield, then start in on the dashboard,
then pry open the guts under the hood to make it stop
and deliver a little message to the slob

who's sleeping in, so hung over he doesn't hear
the sound his ride is broadcasting loud enough
to let all his neighbors know he's out of touch

or out of town or too tone-deaf to care.
There ought to be a law—and, in fact, there is.
But the horn is unconcerned

and will sound off until its battery runs down
sometime next spring, fending off imagined thieves
and summoning vigilantes.

On the Bright Side

Today I thank God for clean glasses—
who knew the world was so bright,
and the thin grass in my yard:

each perky shoot a proclamation.
Shadows in the neighbors' large,
gnarly tree—no doubt an exotic

import from New Zealand—
cling to the bark like dark
but loving spirits, the tangible love
of light for all that grows

solid enough to take up space
in the world. And lest I forget:
The bill collectors all salute me
with a fawning attentiveness

that touches my purse
and prompts me to write them checks,
signed with my own hand,
my monthly love letters to them all.

A Change of Habit

Maybe today is the day—
                             cloudy, damp,
trees in a whispering congregation—
                                  to join
some monastery, old stone and only one topic of conversation,
God, God, God, so much God I'd feel happy
to cancel all my appointments
                               and don
one of the uniforms that says

I have no social network, I do not root for professional
sportsmen or women, and the latest tinny love song
is not reeling through the poorly constructed partitions
of my subpar mansion of self.
                               I will scrub floors for Jesus
and breathe deep for the Buddha and lust only
for the eternal—
                     try to catch it, ever racing ahead
like the fleetest of predators, exploding into the farthest
edge of the edge of God, a dynamic universe,
focus all my yearning there,
                          beyond beyond,
and breathe deep, then answer the next call to prayer
and drive myself insane with my chosen sect's
favorite love song to God—
                       This is the day!
You are such a God! We worship and grow tired,
but will shower in the icy waters of our repetitive
     existence
and see you again later today
                          in the same place,
at the same time, forever here, forever
now,
     forever.

Postmodern

Come dance with me in the Belle Époque
as we imagine it, with penicillin and anesthesia
and modern dental equipment and Demerol,

without the shadow of the next century,
replete with its appalling slaughter of the innocents
in muddy trenches and frigid gulags, without the need

to avoid the clinical language we invent to tidy up
torture and mass murder in its many manifestations.
Just the soft focus in a carefree Renoir,

without the sentimental palette or the peculiar fondness
for wool and bustiers and corsets and too-tight shoes.
Just the champagne of the afternoon, and an aperitif

or two, and three courses of haute cuisine
plus dessert, and this dance without our stumbling feet
or a story about the morning's cold rain or the sunset's

unbearable *tristesse*, just the love that does not question
how it feels if I sleep with your best friend, or,
in these days of gender confusion, you do the same,

or I lose my arm on the job, or we fail to make
December's rent—just you and me in this bubble
outside of history, a short waltz in sunlight.

In the Wings

Sadness waits in the greenroom.
It has no scheduled air time, yet knows the daily
late night show runs out of comedians at midnight,
and the celebrities and floggers of big ideas
are allowed to pitch only one project at a time.

The zany animal acts are limited to one a week,
and headlines written by inattentive copywriters
only draw a brief guffaw. In the wings, the man
who can cry and wring his hands all night, paired
with the woman who weeps so freely you cannot help
reaching out a hand. Once seated as guests,
either one can steal the show and turn the evening

into one long lament of so many losses,
the torture of a thousand cuts,
the plethora of scars to detail and display,
a river washing to the sea, taking whole chunks
of bluffs that seemed unassailable,
battlements of good cheer and health, retreats
for the bright-eyed and erudite, prime real estate,
giving way to an airy silence and the tiny,
distant cries of the dispossessed.

Crackers

Somewhere among the Olmec heads
that weigh ten tons and the axes smooth as water

and the little masks with faces you want to talk to,
if only you could travel—briefly, with a guaranteed

uneventful germ-free return—across the millennia
to admire the chiseled features and perfect

enameled teeth of the living models,
you no longer have to wonder what the subjects

would say to you, because they begin talking,
or mouthing murmurs from their pedestals

and plastic cases, lit from above or below
for maximum dramatic effect. *Crackers*, they say,

through their eyes, in perfect English, the words
emerging from their frozen features.

—That's what we want. Crackers, the gluten-free jobs
with sesame seeds. A slice of cheese. Even a lowly

tortilla would do. And a cup of that fermented juice
whose formula has been lost to the jungle.

Crackers, they all say, lighting the shadows that hover.
The voices have spoken. I am their emissary.

V.

It Never Ends

We must always be trying to write the poem
we don't feel we have the skill or the means
to write.
        —John Berryman

The day so far: still searching for that epic.
Seafaring? Great mystery of the shadowy deep?
Cataclysm? The earth opening beneath my feet?

Only measured stillness slides
from my pencil. The vision of my old friend,
fresh from cataract surgery,

saying he can once again enjoy looking
at stars, "connecting the dots."
The awe of retracing an old riddle, finding north,

breathing the mist of shepherds and astrologers
drawing myths that still live
in petroglyphs etched in the darkness.

Then winter sidles up in one
final billow of breath condensed
to momentary cloud and tells me

to step back inside, away from the crowded brink
of the universe. Bank the fires
and drift off to dream of the clustered Pleiades.

The World Is a Tired Place

That hummingbird out back looks so busy
wrestling with the tiny fuchsia
whose forebears were carted down
from the foothills of the Andes
by some Peruvian botanist
who had dollar signs in his eyes
and just knew he could sell cuttings
to every half-interested gardener on the West Coast.

A little wren with a yellow cap
has been twitching in my half-filled bird bath
like it could flicker moisture through its small handful
of down all day—but my bones tell the truth,
that entropy is the through-line of the universe,
that kingdoms fall after they rise, leaving
many unanswered questions and a few poignant
piles of rubble. The gods, I might suppose,
are huddled like a lazy pod of sea lions

on that pier by the waterfront, cranky slugs
sleeping off a monumental bender, now and then
shifting their weight to bark at an interloper,
then making room for it to haul out and settle
into a shared state of suspended animation.

How Does it Start?

You clean a crockery cup—
scrub it, in fact, obsessively,
no not quite, but with zeal
and attention—

and when it's rinsed
it looks brand new—no,
better than new, renewed,
a plain brown undistinguished mug
of medium stature, compact,

serviceable—and it positively sings
with glee to be reborn,
yodeling in a kitchen choir
about its lovely, ordered life

and the joy of brewing coffee,
nature's wonder drug,
and then the whole kitchen
starts stirring
beneath your fingertips,
purring smoothly as a tiger cat.

Your eyes catch the grain
of the old cutting board,
so happy to be clean and dry,
and the stove stands by
to celebrate the end
of another useful day.

Don't I Know You?

My life has become a rerun, I think,
an old movie on Saturday night—
not so old that the sound is scratchy
or the actors have been colorized—
and yet years have passed, the lead actor looks
so young, the writer has since entered rehab

and now drinks diet Cokes by the caseful and frets
about his unbreakable addiction to nicotine,
but can't convince himself he could still write
without the friendly assistance of Camels

by the pack—now his never-ending reminder
that the Reaper sits in his living room, biding his time
and catching up on *People* magazine, monitoring
the hijinks of the stars who insist on acting out
the morality tale of the familiar evils of fortune and fame:

temptation loitering on the corner
of every block, offering every form of high
on which anyone can make a buck.

Where was I? Back at that old movie,
marveling at its release date, that I saw it
so long ago I can't remember scene, location, or plot.

Laundry

All the philosophers made it.

Plato did not say I only wear
the idea of laundry; this toga needs
no cleaning, for I merely spill

the essence of lamb fat on it;
that splotch of tzatziki
is just a concept.

No, he did the thing too common
among us: shed his toga and left it
for his wife, after many reminders.

Plato, you have an important symposium
on the idea of evil; who will find
your thoughts fresh if you're clad
in smears of moussaka?

He could not argue with her logic,
or the way she twisted her face
when dramatizing her colloquy.

It's what separates us from the beasts.
Some chimps wear vests,
but only their handlers know
when to call it laundry.

To My Hands

Just now I bought a midday jolt
as if sleepwalking, unable
to register anything
about my server
or anything else

except the astonishing
beige stiletto suede boots
mincing out the door
and the self-important flourish
of the mother and daughter
blocking my access to the milk—

but my hands performed elegantly
as needed, a team of prestidigitators
that fished my glasses case
from my Polartec pocket,
snapped the clip-on shades
off my regular frames,
neatly sequestered the clip-ons
and closed the case,

then located my wallet,
coordinated with my mouth
while it blurted out something
about a small coffee
with room for milk,
plucked out two singles,

placed two quarters
in the tip jar, made sure
to zip my wallet back
in my pocket and carried
the fresh hot cup carefully

to the counter, steering it
discreetly around the suede boots
and the mother and daughter
spreading out their tattered
street map right in front of
the thermoses of milk—

bless them and their clueless
clogging of this busy corner,
they may not even know
their way around a bare-bones café—

and all the while my fingers
are ready at a simple cue
to put down the cup—careful,
no spillage please—and,
if called on, open up
my cello case, make a few
adjustments, and play Beethoven.

My Life: The Script Conference

We know we want Peter Fonda for the lead—
    really, the resemblance is uncanny,
the WASPy affect, not to mention
    the history with reefer, and that attitude—
you know, recovering surly punk,
    the world owes him a living,
he's too fucking smart for his own good—

    and we know this is an indie effort,
just aiming for modest box office,
    some minor prizes, maybe a few
notices praising Peter's sense of nuance
    and his generous support of the promising
young newcomer. And we know he's partly
    himself—a has-been, burned his bridges,
got drunk at a cast party and told the wrong
    studio executive to fuck off. But we

still have no plot. I mean, is this a thriller,
    Fonda morphs into Clint Eastwood
without the Dirty Harry smoldering volcano
    righteous assassin look? Or are we going cultural—

aging anthropologist discovers priceless
    pre-Columbian backgammon board
and returns it to its country of origin,
    while becoming a cultural hero and earning
the lasting respect of Penélope Cruz?

Or is he a straight man for someone funny
who will try without success to make him laugh
　　　at life like Zorba and do a half-assed goat dance
over the closing credits? Does he have a preference?
　　　Can we get him on a conference call?

VI.

Eggs

Out walking the dogs, I notice what they're thinking
clear as day. In their modest thought balloons

there hovers an egg—hardboiled and peeled,
glistening and impervious, a glowing white translucence,

such indescribable integrity, a thing the same
in any language, a protein pill like the watery sun

in today's overcast, shining like a blind eye.
Or like the egg I eat at breakfast—no culinary sensation,

A simple hedge against high blood sugar.
The dogs carry the eggs so freely—one to each thought balloon,

a pair of eggs on leash. The eggs shine whitely
at each blade of grass that's sniffed, endorsing

the invisible scent of the world, the passage
of other dogs with their perfect unthought eggs

like serene bubbles on a slow-moving stream,
reflecting everything without knowing it, gliding

on the surface that is the only dimension
they will ever know, or need.

Gangster of Love

The smell of pot wafts through the car window,
    and my nose perks up, wants to follow that dense,
        dark, sweet, resinous funk to its source and take a hit,
breathe deep, envelop itself in a cloud of smoke,
    inhale something to change my night
        into a special occasion, a random excursion

through the cosmic, but it's just a whiff,
    all I can take now, and I breathe deep,
        give the nose a treat, buddy,
pretend you're sniffing in a contact high and drive on,
    on schedule, untroubled, legal, free, and if not
        clean and sober, well, recently washed anyway,

sober for at least a few days, because sobriety
    is like vegetarianism, which I embrace at breakfast,
        and anyway the smoke dissipates in an instant
and then later I tune in the radio and somebody
    on the other end plays Steve Miller's "Livin' in the U. S. A."
        and the whiff of pot floats me all the way back

to my long-dead friend Bart playing me that song,
    which crescendos to Steve Miller crowing
        with unbridled enthusiasm, *Somebody bring me*
a cheeseburger and then hitting a high note so exuberant
    it's hard not to fall down laughing—
        but what I really want to hear is Bart's favorite,

the next cut, "Gangster of Love"—*Yes I'm a gangster,*
      a gangster of love—and I want it without the rest
           of the story when we go our separate ways
and Bart then dies perhaps of the excesses
      of that enthusiasm and I survive with the guilt
           they have a name for, wondering

if being alive is proof that my credentials
      as a gangster were forged, and then I realize
           I'm alone, driving home in a dark city,
sober, reciting Satchel Paige's mantra
      Don't look back, something
           might be gaining on you.

In Excelsis

Early in the afternoon, the angels
drop three pennies in my path,
scuffed reminders of God's love.

I pick them up, yet wonder
why the angels can't just touch me
on the shoulder once,
for luck, or brush my cheek
with feathered fingers.

Some big lug parks his large
black truck behind me
without so much as a nick
on my bumper. He's no saint,
I can tell by the way the sun
reflects off his cue ball head.

The angels counsel
against hate, and I thank them,
but wonder why they can't pause
to sing a chorus, a Kyrie,
a Te Deum, or—

if they're feeling inspired—

a Gratias agimus tibi,
a Gloria, something to set
the day apart
from all the other
tiny miracles
that got me this far.

Girl with the Parole Hearing

*(voice recognition software transposition
of "Girl with a Pearl Earring")*

What to wear? Nothing too sexy, cleavage is out,
but some leg to catch the officer's eye,
no jewelry of any kind, especially anything

an idiot might think is real. Makeup should be light,
some foundation, easy on the mascara,
and avoid perfume. I'm almost a good girl,

no longer inclined to larceny, though it's still easy
to boost some blush or flash my dazzling smile
and filch a few art books to fence around

the corner. Embezzling, though: I don't even think
about it anymore—not such easy money
after all. If I can just skate today, I'll take a break,

have a smoke and maybe look for a job.
I hear casino dealers do just fine, and I've always
looked great under neon. And everybody's

got a hustle there. No hats: definitely no hats.
And heels, but something demure.
A look that says not guilty, but not innocent.

Roy G. Biv

(Red, Orange, Yellow, Green, Blue, Indigo, Violet:
a general science mnemonic for the visible spectrum of light)

I first heard it backward from my grandfather,
the way the old folks tell everything, starting
with now and working back through the old slights,
illnesses, sudden deaths, the last few wars,
the good old days so drenched in sepia,
the wisdom derived from lives like smoke, hovering
in memory. *Vib-gy-or*, he called it, the visible

spectrum, a word from a magic language
that hides under rocks, trickles through moss,
twinkles in the stars, talking in Technicolor.
And later, from my science teacher,
the reverse, a serviceable mnemonic, the name

of somebody like Kilroy, who was here, there,
and everywhere—even a middle initial, a guy who lives
next door and works pumping gas or bagging groceries
or mowing the lawn. Seven colors to say it all,

even the ordinary green of that peaked shade tree
down by the five and ten, catching the morning light.
Mostly now myself I like it backward—*vib-gy-or*—
the way my grandfather said it carefully, with conviction
and a twinkle in his clouded eye, that opalescent moon.

Civics

I noticed the house was on fire,
      so I turned on the air-conditioning.

Then I drew a bath. Cold water, of course.
      I was just about to settle in when somebody

dressed as a fireman put an ax through the door.
      "What's wrong with you," I yelled, "can't you see

I'm busy fighting this fire?" "Run for your life,"
      he screamed, then stomped off toward the attic,

where the fire had already eaten a hole
      in the roof. I can't abide histrionics,

so I scuttled down to the sidewalk.
      "Officer," I said to a passing policeman,

"arrest that man, he's burning my house
      to the ground." "Are you insane?" roared

the cop. "You don't have to get personal,"
      I said, "just do your job."

All Those Years

All those years we had parakeets, I never thought
to speak a word to them. Not the blue one
we gave a name to without asking,

or the green one who used to warble
Hail to the Chief, or the little yellow job
we liked to call Chiquita, though she never

spent an hour south of the border.
And each of them just like the cliché, a canary
in a coal mine, one day broadcasting seed husks,

sharpening that tiny curved beak
on the special stone hooked to the bars,
caroling in E major to itself in the perfectly round

stainless steel mirror; the next day, keeled over
on the newspaper at the bottom of the cage,
the headlines reading *Scandal! Mayhem! Panic!*—

feathers still jewel-like, composed, iridescent.
But something strange happened to their little souls.
Over night, featherless, reduced to the delicious trill

of song, they'd slipped through the bars and flown
the coop. I can hear them now at dawn, roosting
in the neighbor's redwood, singing to the sun.

Thanks to you all, strange little lights
flickering so delicate in the treetop,
trilling in your own language all day long.

Subversive

Because living is a tricky business,
I bless the earth while I can, by morning light, hoping

to emulate the finches flocking in the trellis out back,
an upturned forest of star jasmine and bougainvillea,

shades of green not yet in bloom, where the finches
seem content to perch and sing and fly to another perch

with no pattern I can discern, announcing daylight,
affirming all that has led me to watch them in their busywork,

the instant embrace of any available branch,
the glide through sunlight, the song of no occasion.

VII.

Sabbath

It's Sunday, putz: day of rest,
not sloth. Bestir thyself, good sir,
at least enough to twist
a wan smile as offering
for the bells cascading
through the neighborhood,
free of any dogma,
like chips of sunshine.

Oh joy, that sound,
right on schedule, proclaiming
something solemn and high,
filled with peace.
An interlude to listen in
on the invisible and its many
chiming permutations,

a moment of wonder
without apology, something
to decorate the silence,
followed then by silence
itself—now humming
with resonance. This is good;
yes: This *is* good.

That One

Suffering speaks no single language,
though I wonder sometimes about Latin,
the medical tongue, and maybe even financial talk
worldwide, with its bloodless fondness
for bankruptcy, foreclosure, and hunger.

Suffering seems to hover over the destitute,
those who say the word *food* in any language
the way the rich say *polo ponies*, with delicious
anticipation, or *Caribbean* when they can pause
for effect and add *vacation*.

Today, I too have the luxury of imagining suffering,
of turning away from all languages that ache
or cry in pain or want with a desire so pure
it takes your breath away.

Today I only wish to please the fates,
to praise the busy village of my body,
to love goldenrod, to admire the pollinators
working to save their acre of the earth,

and hope the dark trinity pauses
for a moment to say *That one:*
He still pleases us. Let him live.

The World since Yesterday

For my father

You keep him alive with longing and regret,
memory a patient spider lashing
the once living to that yesterday when his story stopped

and you became one of those spirits divorced
from morning sun, riding an iceberg
calved from the land, looking shoreward at dusk.

The metaphors are pretty, though sad,
and all the cells of your aching body feel only sad,
and you are a wobbling top

running down, axis more and more uncertain,
someone cast out in a foreign land
unable to say even Help me, I'm standing

on sand in the face of a rising tide, I am bereft
and alone, however you might say that
in your unfamiliar tongue, I am too tired to weep,

too late to save anyone, a sack of skin and bones
arattle, no one on earth to point me home, no home
in what is known, the rest past words, unknown.

A Rising Tide

lifts all boats, they say—the yachtsmen,
the commanders of navies—ignoring
the requirements of metaphor,
that the words look past the epigram

to those who sit in boats stove in,
those who have abandoned ship to watch
from shore as their crafts sink
under the weight of crushing freight,
their hulls no longer buoyant. And those unable
to launch so much as a dinghy.

Consider those faced by rising tides:
inundation, the loss of shoreline,
the ravages of hurricane and monsoon.

Who can blame the rich for choosing a metaphor
they can embrace as if it were truth?
But still you hope that those fretting
on the decks of sinking ships
could be towed to shore, those burdened
by cargo could be helped to lighten their load,
that the masses denied travel by yacht
could enjoy at least some ferry service.

That poetry could be put in its proper place: not the tool
of legislators who can't scan a line. Not a shaper
of policy. What we turn to after the boat goes down.

A Drink with Billy Collins

I try to keep it casual, something like a collegial outing
from the days when I could wear those elbow patches
on my sports coat and make jokes about Shelley over sherry

without getting my tongue twisted up in the delivery—
Hail to thee, blithe rabbit! Bird thou never wert!
I invite my wife to keep the conversation flowing

while we wait for our measure of gin or vodka
or my sheepish choice of a moderately priced
California sauvignon blanc, and she tells him

all about the days of long ago when Bruno,
the world's most dyspeptic bartender, kicked us
out of his bar, a Haight Street novelty dive called

Aub Zam Zam, a pretty, horseshoe-shaped bar,
and a reputation for the best martinis in town.
I watch the poet's professorial eyes narrow a bit,

his mouth purse in a tight smile, and we both marvel
at her acid and inventive invocation of Bruno,
for a moment brought back to life to say

Out! Out! That's it! The bar is closed!

My Life in Translation

Born helpless. Thrived, to a degree. Grew faster
than a redwood for a while. Gained some skills
to help read the signs. Took a few

nasty falls. Moved, at last, to Liechtenstein.
So tiny, just a patch of dirt. It has no navy,
fewer divisions than the Pope, offers

no strategic advantage, and—unlike the hardy Swiss—
has no ring of frozen Alps to protect it.
In discussions of global strategy, no one turns

to its ambassador with furrowed brow
and asks, *How say the people of Liechtenstein?*
It lives in peace because it can wage no war;

sends beggars to the Dutch,
budding socialists to the French,
and brooding fascists across the border

to Germany. Few wish to visit, either to take in
the vistas of small, flat landscapes, or to work
in its major light industry, the making of colorful stamps.

Its engravers tell little stories that people stick
in dust-covered albums: the history of flowers;
castles on the Rhine; potato fields of northern France;

clarets of the Somme. All squeezed
into a frame the size of your thumb—beautiful
yet humble, perfectly composed, easy to overlook.

My Five Minutes with Jesus

Lord, I've thought a lot about this interlude. I'm dazzled
and adore you and thank you for your house call,
but let's get down to business. First, I've got some
aches and pains. Will decline to specify: you know

the ones. Just pass your magic fingers
through my aura or whatever you do
and set my body free. And now: Could we start
with water into wine? If you could anoint me

as your acolyte, I believe there's money
in this trick. Beaujolais, burgundy, merlot, zinfandel,
no matter, so long as the quality makes people
raise their glasses in your name and dance

past midnight. Time left? What about Lazarus,
can you raise me up someone of his ilk,
still fresh, because I think you missed a chance
to secure a very grateful servant, one who

would gladly paint my house and mow the lawn
for an eternity. And this walking on water:
I don't need to cross an ocean, but if you could
let me navigate a large lake on my pedal extremities

I'd be happy to claim a listing in The Guinness Book.
Still a minute left? Can you tell me who's got the bits
of the true cross, and your genuine foreskin?
And what's with the Shroud of Turin?

One last request: a few fingernail clippings. Make them
undeniably authentic, maybe glow in the dark,
or with the Lord's Prayer (your handiwork, remember?)
etched in Aramaic on each tiny sliver. Amen.

Nixon in Heaven

I can still smell the lilies at my funeral—lush, sweet,
abundant, the scent swirling in among the pops
of the twenty-one gun salute, all those fine
young marines in white gloves—and the eulogies to me,
a statesman. That's all I ever really wanted.

Now I'm an unknown—surprised, really,
to be here at all, but it's not as if they've put me in charge,
though I did put in one request to oversee
surveillance. I'm in a little shack at The Outskirts—
that's what they call it, it's a big, lonely district—

and I've got a piano. I'm learning *Hail to the Chief*,
some variations I'm working up myself.
Liberace comes by to help me with my technique.
He wears tails that light up like stars and stripes,
and he tells me soon I'll be ready for the dancing waters.

Pat stops by too—part of her therapy, I gather.
She calls me a son of a bitch and a miserable
cocksucker, then grins and pats my cheek.
Leaving, she slams the door so hard the roof wobbles,
then floats off with the most endearing spring in her step.

VIII.

Self-Portrait

My photo: always a surprise. Unwelcome as a bum sleeping
on my doorstep, the one who stole my paper and then took

a nice, long relaxing leak on my front door, causing a gentle
rivulet of pee to drip down into the garage. This after I thoughtfully

declined to roust him when I opened the door for the paper.
Take my new license photo: I can't believe I'm the cranky

old bastard with the saggy jowls and thin hair who looks like
he's ready for the local cursing contest, ready to blaspheme

on any available topic, then shuffle home and write outraged
letters to the editor all morning on the lamentable state

of everything in the world, including the unfortunate proliferation
of dwarves and midgets in TV advertising and the thin,

expressionless tone of the symphony's oboe section.
Still, a step up from last time, when I looked like the village idiot.

Given a chance, I'd still send myself packing and set off
in search of that polymath matinee idol living in my skin.

Postcard from California

Sun goes down on another useless day
without seeming to care. That's California for you:
hard to get the weather to take things seriously.

Even a killing drought is just sunshine all day long.
Citizens of all ages on the tennis courts
with their Day-Glo green balls, *pock, pock, pock,*

working up a healthy sweat, drinking
that bottled water laced with polysyllabic additives
to extend their lives past one hundred.

God, what I wouldn't give for a hurricane
to furrow their brows, make them watch
the barometer fall. The little children are the worst,

like the neighbor's across the street, shouting
and skipping like nobody's told them
about the national debt, or the bands of hostiles

lurking in those foreign mountains waiting
to skewer them all. No dark prospect
of a long winter to put a damper on the populace.

Maybe I'm homesick for lands where nothing works
and everything matters, where life is a series of Pyrrhic victories
and all roads lead to February's soot-covered snow.

Wings to Fly

I guess I'd hover
over the neighborhood,
inspect rooftops,
light for a moment
on the tip of the neighbors' redwood
but not rest long unless
I had a really fine song
to show off to the residents,
a fancy trill mixed with a tidy run,
a high note not of ecstasy
but the easy grace with which
the birds praise the sky,
bright and airy.

Then some soaring,
nothing too extreme,
a short glide north
to sanctuary, a forest of ancients,
mist hanging in meditation,
the stillness of centuries woven
as tapestry and stretched
tree to tree. After that,

ascent to the little grove
atop the hill looking down
on the city, the hustle
and rush muted
by miles. The only sound
the breath of a west wind
easing through a circle
of evergreens.

Nature-Lover

First thing, I stop by the small lily pond to view the frog
that lives there, to check each lily pad,

variegated and fancy, some sporting flowers, one
purple, the other white, also carrying of course

all the lore of the lily, the Buddhist tales I think,
but I bypass all the stories about the lilies

growing up through the mud, the way the spirit flowers
after ascending through so many layers of muck.

I check all the pads carefully, thinking of my friend Farley
and our days kayaking in the Pamet River,

when he would drift a moment and then snatch a frog
out of the shadows, like a magician, and he would say

Don't you see them, to which I could always honestly answer
No, except a time or two. He'd hold the captive up

by a twitching rear leg and pose a moment, triumphant,
then throw it back, to disappear and hide in what one suspects

must be the amphibian version of abject terror, eyes a-bug.
Even after trolling through all the wisdom narratives

and thoughts of Farley posing in triumph, after
checking each lily pad in hopes of repeating the one

single solitary sighting of this frog, who was perched
on a pad that couldn't really support him—or her,

I don't know how to sex a frog—but he didn't care,
he just sat on the pad in need of bailing out, amphibious,

perhaps happy, still, silent, unconcerned about
the smallness of his pond, not bemoaning his lack

of a mate, with what appeared to be no concern for me
or my wife, or whether he'd had a good morning

catching mosquitoes—even after all that, I saw
no frog. And so I filled the rest of my walk with the part

only we humans can manage—after the simple
binary experience of seeing or not seeing, hearing

or not hearing, noting or failing to note—which is the part
where I wonder about the frog's state of mind,

and his origins, and admire his composed silence.
I imagine him at the bottom of the pond, and wonder

what time he surfaces, because he must, and if I want to wake
at 6 to take an early-morning look, or if it matters

whether I see the frog or not, because after all it is
just a frog. But it's a story, too, of something small

and easy to pass by, alien and fascinating, living
a life I will never understand from the distance at which

I view him, if I view him, when I view him, before
moving on to other things, like the guy with the t-shirt

reading *Nobody* in sketchy letters, which leaves me wondering
if he has a matching one that says *Somebody*

in the same sketchy letters. I also note
that the frog would not care which shirt this fellow

was wearing, and couldn't read any part of either one,
and probably won't even ever see the road

this guy was walking along, and doesn't know
I was looking for him this morning, standing for a moment

by his pond, silent, scanning, looking for something
I didn't see, but will look for again tomorrow.

About the Author

Will Walker was born and raised in Boston, Massachusetts, and spent his summers on Cape Cod, in Provincetown. He moved to San Francisco in 1973 after exhausting all other options and has lived there since. He lives in the Haight with his wife, Valerie, and their spirited Chihuahua.

His poetry has appeared in *Across Borders, Alabama Literary Review, Alimentum, Bark, Burningwood, Chagrin River Review, The Chiron Review, Conch.es, Crack the Spine, Diverse Arts Project, Forge, The Haight Ashbury Literary Journal, Hartskill Review, Lame Duck, Passager, Pennsylvania English, Spillway Review, Street Sheet, Red Hills Review, Rougarou, Schyulkill Valley Journal of the Arts, Slow Trains, Spillway Review, Street Sheet, Street Spirit, Studio One,* and *WriterAdvice*.

As a general summary of his life, he currently embraces these words from Berndt Oksendal's *Stochastic Differential Equations: An Introduction with Applications*:

We have not succeeded in answering all our problems. The answers we have found only serve to raise a whole set of new questions. In some ways we feel we are as confused as ever, but we believe we are confused on a higher level, and about more important things.

www.ingramcontent.com/pod-product-compliance
Lightning Source LLC
Chambersburg PA
CBHW022200080426
42734CB00006B/521